"Hey A.I." - You N' A.I. IRL

Raymond Amari

Copyright © 2023 Raymond Amari

All rights reserved

No part of this book may be reproduced, or stored in a retrieval system, or transmitted in any form or by any means, electronic, mechanical, photocopying, recording, or otherwise, without express written permission of the publisher.

"Hey A.I." - You N' A.I. IRL was created and dictated by Raymond Amari. Typed, checked and edited by an A.I. system created and trained by Raymond Amari.

For my wonderful parents for always supporting my love of computers, even if Dad thinks I'll create Terminators one day...

CONTENTS

Title Page

Copyright

Dedication

"Hey A.I.!" - You N' A.I. IRL　　　　　　　　　　　　　　　　1

Introduction: The Age of Collaboration　　　　　　　　　　2

Chapter 1: A Quick History of A.I. (Robots Weren't Always as Smart as they were on TV)　　　4

Chapter 2: A.I. in Pop Culture vs. Reality (Spoiler: It's Not as Scary as in the Movies)　　　7

Chapter 3: Humans at the Center of A.I. Development (Yes, We're Still the Boss)　　　11

Chapter 4: A.I. in Daily Life (It's Everywhere and You Probably Didn't Even Notice)　　　15

Chapter 5: The Workplace of Tomorrow (Spoiler Alert: It's Not Full of Robots Yet)　　　20

Chapter 6: Enhancing Human Creativity with A.I. (Because Two Heads Are Better Than One)　　　24

Chapter 7: A.I. in Scientific Discovery and Research (Your New Lab Partner)　　　28

Chapter 8: A.I. Augmenting Human Abilities (A Superpower for Everyone)　　　32

Chapter 9: A.I. and Ethics—Navigating Challenges Together　　　35

(Because Even Superpowers Need Rules)

Chapter 10: The Emotional and Creative Dimensions of A.I. (Can A.I. Feel?)   39

Chapter 11: Education in the A.I. Age (A.I. in the Classroom: A+ or Needs Improvement?)   43

Chapter 12: A.I. for Good: Social Impact and Sustainability (Saving the World, One Algorithm at a Ti   48

Chapter 13: The Limits and Dangers of Artificial Intelligence - Do Not Do That Alone!   53

Chapter 14: Societal Trust and Human-A.I. Relationships (How to Be Friends with A.I.)   58

Chapter 15: Embracing the Unknown Together (The Journey Ahead)   62

Chapter 16: The Real Life Stories of A.I. Changing the World   65

Chapter 17: Bonus! Fun and Simple A.I. Projects You Can Try (No PhD Required!)   71

With thanks!   75

About The Author   77

"HEY A.I.!" - YOU N' A.I. IRL

(Dictated) By Raymond Amari

('Technically' written, checked and corrected by A.I. because Ray hates editing!)

INTRODUCTION: THE AGE OF COLLABORATION

Imagine you live in a world where robots and humans work together, not in some far-off future, but, like, right now. Maybe you think of A.I. (Artificial Intelligence) as only really possible in sci-fi movies or cartoons, where robots have minds of their own, take over the world, fall in love with humans or drink heavily and shirk their responsibilities. But, in reality, A.I. is already all around us. It's in your cell phone, helping you get directions and in the background of your favorite app, recommending songs, videos and products you didn't even know you needed.

Don't worry - A.I. isn't here to steal your job or turn you into a science experiment. It's here to make life easier, faster and more interesting. Whether it's helping doctors spot diseases more quickly, powering self-driving cars, or even just making your playlists smarter, A.I. is becoming our partner in everyday tasks. A partnership that is only growing stronger and better for us both.

So, what's this book about? It's about how we, humans (assuming you are human, the truth is out there after all) can work with A.I. to make our lives better. Not just in big, world-changing ways, but also in like, small, everyday ways. It's not about A.I. taking over the world, it's about A.I. and us teaming up, each doing what we're best at.

This book will take you on a journey from the history of A.I. to how it's changing the way we live and work today. We'll explore what A.I. really is (and what it's not), how it helps in like, creative or practical tasks and stuff, but, most importantly, how it makes us better at what we do.

By the end of this book, you'll hopefully see that A.I. isn't something to fear. Instead, it's like the best bro you could ever have - like, super smart, always there when you need them and ready to handle all the lame, boring stuff so you can focus on being awesome.

So let's dive in and see how humans and A.I. can work together, creating a future that's full of possibility (and way fewer repetitive tasks)!

CHAPTER 1: A QUICK HISTORY OF A.I. (ROBOTS WEREN'T ALWAYS AS SMART AS THEY WERE ON TV)

A.I. might seem like a new thing, but humans have been dreaming of robots and smart machines for a way, way long time. Like, way before your phone started learning what kind of pizza you like to order on Friday nights.

The Early Days: When Machines Were Just a Dream

Believe it or not, the idea of machines thinking like humans goes all the way back to like, ancient history times. Philosophers like Aristotle (yes, the dude from ancient Greece) wondered how humans think and if machines could maybe do the same stuff. Of course, Aristotle didn't have Netflix recommendations or self-checkout machines, but the seeds of A.I. were already there in his head.

Fast forward like, a couple of thousand years and you've got people like Alan Turing, a British mathematician in the 1940s, asking a huge question: "Can machines think?" Turing didn't just ask this for the lols; he went ahead and started figuring out how machines might be able to solve problems on their own. He even came up with something called the 'Turing Test', which is still used today to see if a machine can fool people into thinking it's human.

Back then, computers weren't all that smart. They took up entire rooms and mostly just crunched numbers. If you asked one to order pizza for you, it would probably just blow a big-ass fuse.

The 1950s: Let's Get This (A.I.) Party Started!

The term 'artificial intelligence' was officially born in 1956, thanks to a bunch of like, really smart folks at Dartmouth College, who wanted to figure out if machines could really learn and think like we do. This was the start of A.I. as a serious field of research. Their quest? To teach machines to solve problems like the way humans do, like with planning, reasoning and stuff like that. Maybe they could teach it to even win a game of chess.

Early A.I. was pretty vanilla and basic. Computers could do things like play simple games or solve math problems, but they couldn't do much else. Still, this was a massive thing at the time! It was like giving a calculator a tiny bit of human-like thinking power.

However, just like when you start a new hobby or a game or something and get frustrated when you're not like, a boss at it immediately, A.I. hit some bumps in the road. In the 1970s and 1980s, people realized that teaching machines to think was way harder than they had expected it would be. They called this the "A.I. Winter" because progress slowed down and the excitement around A.I. cooled off.

The 2000s: A.I. Learns to Be Smart (Finally)

After like a few decades of trying and failing, A.I. finally got a boost in the 2000s. What changed? Three big things: computers got faster, there was more data and the algorithms got better (basically, smarter ways to teach machines stuff). This combination meant that A.I. could finally start doing actual useful things, like recognizing your face in a photo or understanding what you mean when you ask your phone to find the nearest coffee shop.

Suddenly, A.I. wasn't just like a science experiment anymore - it was part of everyday life. Companies started using A.I. to recommend what movie you should watch, what products you should buy and even how to drive your car. If you've ever kicked back and let an app do the dull thinking stuff for you, congratulations, you've already got an A.I.

teammate.

Today: A.I. Everywhere

Now we live in a world where A.I. is like, everywhere. It's not just about robots in labs or machines playing chess anymore. A.I. is helping doctors find diseases early, assisting scientists in researching climate change and yes, helping you figure out what song to play next on your playlist.

But here's the best part: A.I. is working alongside humans in ways that like, make both of us better. We bring the creativity and judgment, A.I. brings the speed and power to analyze huge amounts of information and together, we can do things faster, smarter and better than either of us could going solo. So, while A.I. isn't quite the robot overlord that some people fear (or kinda hoped for), it is a powerful tool that's becoming a bigger part of our lives every day.

CHAPTER 2: A.I. IN POP CULTURE VS. REALITY (SPOILER: IT'S NOT AS SCARY AS IN THE MOVIES)

If you've ever watched a movie that was made in the last 50 years (if you're that vintage or just like the old stuff), chances are you've seen A.I. portrayed in all kinds of mental ways. Sometimes, A.I. is the helpful sidekick (like in Iron Man) and other times, it's the villain trying to kill us all (anyone remember Terminator?), but how close are these movie robots to real-life A.I.?

Spoiler alert: Not very.

A.I. in Movies: The Good, the Bad and the Completely Unrealistic

Let's start with the 'Good'. In movies like Iron Man or Star Wars, A.I. is often shown as a helpful, reliable squadmate. Think about J.A.R.V.I.S., Tony Stark's A.I. buddy that runs his entire superhero suit, or my boy R2D2 in Star Wars. J.A.R.V.I.S. knows what Tony wants before he even asks while R2 saves the day over and over with just a few beeps. It's like having the ultimate personal assistant who can fight bad guys, unlock doors and manage your calendar.

Then there's the 'Bad' side. In movies like The Matrix or the previously mentioned Terminator (my Dad's favorite film), A.I. is shown as the enemy - super smart machines plotting to enslave us or to simply like, kill us. Think about those squid-like robots in The Matrix - hunting us down, plugging us into a computer program and then using us as batteries.

So, what's the truth? Is A.I going to be your best friend or your worst nightmare? Well, the reality is that A.I in movies is, at least for now, 'Completely Unrealistic'. Here, in the real world, A.I is a lot less drama and a load more practical.

A.I. in Real Life: Smarter Than You Think (But Not Quite J.A.R.V.I.S.)

In real life, A.I. isn't a villain or a superhero, it's just a set of smart tools we can use to make our lives like, a million times easier. Think about it - when you ask Siri to send a text, or use Google Maps to find the fastest way home, you're using A.I. It's not plotting anything; it's just processing data to help you out.

Here's what A.I. can really do:

Help you make decisions: We all kinda suck when it comes to making the difficult decisions in life, like what to watch. A.I. can analyze data and offer recommendations, like Netflix suggesting shows you'll probably love (even if you're not proud of your binge-watching choices).

Make life more convenient: Smart assistants like Alexa can turn on the lights, play your favorite music, or even order you that pizza (probably with extra cheese, if it knows you well enough).

Solve big problems: A.I. is being used in hospitals to help doctors diagnose diseases faster, in factories to make production more efficient and in science labs to figure out tough problems like climate change.

But here's what A.I can't do (at least not yet):

Feel emotions: No, your A.I. assistant isn't throwing shade at you for ignoring its advice and it also isn't just chilling. A.I. straight up doesn't have feelings.

Think like a human: A.I. can process huge amounts of information really fast and it might seem super smart, but it doesn't have creativity or intuition the way that us humans do. It can tell you the weather, the time, even the name of the song playing that you like, just can't figure out, but it won't write you a poem (unless you teach it to, but that's a whole other story).

Take over the world: Sorry, Terminator fans (yes Dad, I mean you!). A.I. can't make decisions on its own outside of the stuff it's programmed to do - it needs humans to tell it what to do. For now, world domination is still firmly in our hands (and possibly aliens).

The Real Magic: When Humans and A.I. Team Up

The real power of A.I. isn't about robots taking over; it's about what happens when humans and A.I. work together. Think of A.I. as like, a super-smart assistant. It can do math, check out trends and figure out patterns faster than we ever could, because it isn't having to use brainpower on more important stuff, like how to beat that guy on COD that you're pretty sure is cheating, or what you're going to have for dinner (I've got such a craving for pizza!), but it still needs humans to guide it, to ask the right questions and figure out what to do with all that information.

Take the healthcare industry, for example. A.I. can analyze thousands and thousands of medical images to help doctors detect early signs of disease, but it's still the doctors, like, regular human doctors, who make the final call. A.I. isn't replacing doctors; it's giving them more tools to work with.

In creative fields, like music, writing or art, A.I. can help spark a new idea, check and edit the stuff we dictate (thank you A.I, I hate having to do it myself) or generate cool patterns, but it's us humans who add the soul and meaning to the things we create. A.I. might be able to write a catchy jingle, but it can't create a masterpiece that moves people to tears (well, not yet anyway - some of it is pretty good, but it isn't on our level). The custom one I'm using right now for dictating this book **should** be typing it out exactly as I speak it, but I have a screen handy to highlight things (like 'should' earlier in this sentence) because, at the end of the day, this is my creation and A.I. can't always understand intention or tone.

So, when you see A.I. in the movies, remember that while it makes for great entertainment to chill out to, real-life A.I. is all about making life smoother, faster and more awesome.

CHAPTER 3: HUMANS AT THE CENTER OF A.I. DEVELOPMENT (YES, WE'RE STILL THE BOSS)

I've talked about how A.I. is all around us, but here's the thing that often gets overlooked: humans are still in control. In fact, without us, A.I. wouldn't exist at all. We've built A.I., we teach it what to do and we decide what stuff it does. A.I. might be smart, but we're smarterer! We're the ones with the creativity, intuition and big-picture thinking. So don't worry, we're still in charge.

Building A.I.: It Starts with Us

Every piece of A.I., from the simple algorithms that suggest what song to play next to the way more complex systems used in self-driving cars, is designed and built by people. A.I. isn't some crazy magical thing that just appeared one day and it's not being built by other robots - it's the result of years of human work, research and imagination.

Think of A.I. like some tool. Just like a hammer needs a person to swing it, A.I. needs humans to program it and give it direction. Even the smartest A.I. in the world can't do anything unless a human sets it in motion.

Here's how humans are involved every step of the way:

Designing A.I. systems: It all starts with people figuring out what it is they want A.I. to do. This could be anything from recognizing speech (so we can dictate a book on A.I. for example) to recommending the best pizza toppings. Once they know what they want, programmers and engineers get to work designing a system that can do the thing.

Training A.I.: A.I. learns by looking at examples. Let's say we want A.I. to recognize pictures of dogs. We need to show it like, thousands, maybe even millions, of dog pictures and then tell it, "Yep, that's a dog" or "Nah man, that's a cat." Over time, the A.I. gets better at telling the difference, but it's humans who provide all the training.

Guiding A.I.'s decisions: Even after an A.I. system is built and trained, it still needs humans to tell it how it's used. If an A.I. system suggests some new merch for you to buy, it's because humans set the rules about what makes a good recommendation.

We're Teaching A.I. to Be Smarter (But Not to Be Human)

A.I. is smart, but it's not 'human-smart'. What does that mean? Well, A.I. can process a ton of information really super fast and recognize patterns in data better than most humans, but it doesn't understand things like the way that we do. It doesn't have common sense or intuition - it does what the programming tells it to do and it can't think creatively without some major help from us.

For example, A.I. can be really good at diagnosing medical conditions by analyzing thousands of x-rays, but it can't decide what treatment is best for a patient. That decision requires things like a doctor's knowledge, judgment, experience and ability to understand human things like emotions, pain and patient preferences.

So, when we teach A.I., we're not trying to turn it into a human. Instead, we're teaching it to do specific things, like things that humans don't have the time, energy, desire or sheer brainpower to do. It's like having an assistant that can handle the heavy brain-lifting while we focus on the stuff that only humans can do.

Humans Make the Rules

Since we're the ones creating and teaching A.I., we also get to make the rules. We decide how A.I. behaves, what it's allowed to do and what kinds of decisions it can make. Think of it like your parents and you, except you're a supercomputer and instead of asking for the car keys, you're analyzing data faster than you can blink.

Here are some examples of how humans control A.I.:

Setting limits: A.I. can't just do like, whatever it wants, whenever it chooses. Programmers put strict limits on what A.I. is allowed to do. For example, a self-driving car's A.I. can't decide to randomly go off-road or choose to go out for pizza, unless it's been programmed to handle that (most aren't).

Ethical guidelines: We also set ethical boundaries for A.I. - that means we decide what's fair, safe and appropriate when it comes to A.I. decisions. Companies and governments are working on guidelines to make sure A.I. isn't biased or unfair, especially in areas like hiring or criminal justice.

Updating A.I.: A.I. isn't a one-and-done deal. Humans are constantly updating and improving A.I. systems to fix mistakes and make them better. If an A.I. system is making bad recommendations or isn't working well, humans go in and tweak it.

The Future of A.I. Depends on Us

As A.I. gets more and more advanced, some people are starting to worry that like, it might start to take over or something. But here's the truth: A.I. can only do what we tell it to do. It doesn't have its own goals, desires or motivations. It's just a tool - an incredibly powerful tool, but still just a tool, so everyone can chill.

So, the future of A.I.? That's up to us. We're the ones who decide how A.I will be used, what problems it will solve and how it will fit into our daily lives and stuff. The great news is that as long as we keep humans in the loop, A.I. will continue to be a tool that helps us, not replaces us.

TL/DR:

At the end of the day, A.I. is a team effort and humans are the team captains. We build A.I., we teach it and we make the rules about how it behaves. A.I. may be smart, but without human creativity, intuition and judgment, it wouldn't be nearly as useful. So, next time you hear someone say, "A.I. is going to take over the world," or like, some other drama, just remember: we're still the ones in charge and we're using A.I. to make life better, not scarier.

CHAPTER 4: A.I. IN DAILY LIFE (IT'S EVERYWHERE AND YOU PROBABLY DIDN'T EVEN NOTICE)

Here's the funny thing about A.I.: it's probably all around you and you didn't even realize it. From the moment you wake up and check your phone, to when you order dinner with just a few clicks, A.I. is quietly lurking working in the background. It's not flashy and it's definitely not trying to take over the world. Instead, A.I. is helping with the little things, making everyday life a little bit easier, one algorithm at a time.

A.I. in Your Pocket, but Not a Pocket Monster!: Smartphones and Smart Assistants

Let's start with the device you probably have with you 24/7, something you might even be using right now - your phone. Your smartphone is basically like a pocket-sized A.I. machine, packed with apps and features that make your life easier. Every time you use:

Voice Assistants (like Siri, Alexa, or Google Assistant): That is A.I. understanding your voice, figuring out what it is that you want and responding. It's also learning from you, remembering that you like your alarms set for 7 a.m. (urgh, mornings, am I right?) or that you're like, always asking for directions to the nearest coffee shop.

Photo Organizers: A.I. is behind the magic that groups your photos into albums and even creates videos of your favorite moments. It doesn't know what's happening in your life, obvi, but it's smart enough to identify patterns, organize your memories and stuff.

Ever wondered how your phone predicts the next word you want to type in your texts? That's A.I., too. If your autocorrect keeps changing 'you're' to 'your' well, let's just say A.I. isn't perfect, but it's getting better like, every day.

Shopping with A.I.: "You Might Also Like…"

When you shop online, you've probably seen those recommendations like 'Customers who bought this also bought…' That's A.I. in action. It's checking out your shopping habits, figuring out what stuff is popular with people like you and then giving you suggestions to buy stuff you didn't even know you needed. It's why I now have a pinball machine in the living room and a big credit card bill.

When you browse streaming sites like Netflix, A.I. is hard at work recommending movies and shows based on what you've watched. It's the same thing when you scroll through Amazon or even when Spotify creates a playlist just for you. A.I. is learning your preferences and helping you discover things you might love (let's be honest, it's programmed to suggest things you're likely to spend money on).

It's kind of like shopping with a buddy who knows like, all your favorite things, except this friend is pushing hard for you to spend those hard-earned dollars! Also, they have a database of like, millions of people's shopping habits and knows exactly what's trending.

Smart Homes: A.I., Butler Style

Ever asked Alexa to turn off the lights to set the mood for some Netflix time? That's A.I. giving you the experience of having one of those things only fancy people used to have - a butler. From adjusting your lights to managing your appliances, A.I.-powered smart home devices give you the life you've only seen on Downton and all you gotta do is say what you want. You barely have to lift a finger, although you may need to like, shout or repeat yourself sometimes!

Some other popular smart home devices examples include:

Smart thermostats (like Nest): They automatically learn how you like your temperature and when, automatically adjusting the temperature in your home based on your preferences. You don't have to worry about coming home to like, a freezing cold house in winter. A.I.'s got your back man, it's all good.

Security cameras: A.I. can detect movement, recognize familiar faces and send you alerts when something unusual happens. They're also responsible for some unexpected funny videos!

Fridges: It still feels a little weird that you can talk with your fridge. A.I. managed fridges can tell you when you're getting low on stuff, with some even able to place an order from the store. Now there'll be two of you wondering what you're looking for when you just open the door and just stare inside.

Transportation: A.I. on the Road

A.I. is also driving us - literally. Self-driving cars, while still in development, rely heavily on A.I. to navigate roads, avoid obstacles and make decisions in real time. These cars use sensors, cameras and literally loads of data to figure out the best route and avoid accidents. We're not quite at the stage where every car on the road is self-driving, but companies like Tesla and Google's Waymo are working on it.

Even if you're not in a self-driving car yet, because they're super expensive and maybe you have a massive credit card bill to pay off, A.I. is still helping you get from A to B. Apps like Google Maps and Waze use A.I. to predict traffic conditions, give you the fastest routes and can even tell you when you should head off to avoid all the traffic. A.I. might make a good passenger to have riding shotgun, plotting a route and like, controlling the tunes, but make sure you stay observant behind the wheel as A.I. can make mistakes!

A.I. in Healthcare: Keeping You Healthy

Healthcare is one of the most important areas where A.I. is making a massive difference. While your doctor probably isn't a robot (at least, not yet), A.I. is already helping doctors make faster and way more accurate diagnoses. Here's how:

Medical imaging: A.I. can analyze X-rays, M.R.I.s and a bunch of other scans faster than any human, helping doctors spot diseases like cancer earlier than they could on their own.

Predictive healthcare: A.I. can predict potential health risks by analyzing data from your medical history. It can track data and search for patterns much quicker than a regular doc and can even take into account your parent's records and stuff like that.

In the future, A.I. could play an even bigger role in helping doctors make better, quicker decisions, offer treatments that are custom for you and maybe even find cures for diseases we're still battling today.

A.I. Behind the Scenes: Making the World Work

While we see A.I. in our personal gadgets and apps, some of the most impressive A.I. work happens behind the scenes, where we don't even notice it. For example:

Banking and finance: A.I. is used to detect fraudulent transactions in real time. Ever get a text from your bank asking if it was really you who just spent $2000 on a pinball machine? That's A.I. watching your back. That said, I also got the same messages from my roommate and my mom...

Customer service: Chatbots are the unrecognized heroes of a load of websites. When you get help with like, your cable bill maybe, or even like, an insurance claim, from a friendly online assistant, you're probably chatting with an A.I. chatbot. Who wants to make an actual phone call if they don't have to? These bots can answer common questions, solve problems and save humans for the tricky issues.

Tl/DR:
A.I. is everywhere, it's pretty helpful and it is here to stay. From the apps we use daily to the cars we drive and even the healthcare we receive - it might not have the drama we might expect from robots working in our world, but it's quietly making our lives easier, safer and more efficient. Whether it's helping you find your favorite TV show (or something like it), keeping an eye on your home, or making sure your next doctor's visit goes without an issue, A.I. is part of your team, even if you didn't realize it.

The best part? It's getting better every day.

CHAPTER 5: THE WORKPLACE OF TOMORROW (SPOILER ALERT: IT'S NOT FULL OF ROBOTS YET)

The workplace is evolving. Big old factory machinery clanking away slowly became fast, technology-powered sites while rows of people sitting at desks became bustling offices, arranged with cubicles. Time has changed a lot and even more changed after the pandemic. Workplaces are now more 'fluid' than ever. However, while it's tempting to imagine that we're a small step from a workplace where robots handle all the boring tasks and humans just sit back and chill, that's not exactly what's happening. Sure, A.I. is changing how we work and factories are now mostly automated,, but instead of replacing us, A.I. is teaming up with us. We might not be able to sit back and chill, but in a lot of cases, we're at least safer.

How A.I. Is Transforming Jobs (Assistance in disguise!)

A.I. isn't just for the million tech companies that seem to make up most of California, nor is it just for like, futuristic factories. It's already being used in all kinds of jobs, from finance to marketing to healthcare. No, it's not here to take your job, it has no desires or ulterior motives. More likely, it's here to help you do your job better (and maybe even faster).

Here are some ways A.I. is changing different industries:

Finance: When I was a little kid my mom had this little book she carried everywhere and would pay at stores with a page from it. It was so weird. I now know that this was something called a 'checkbook' and every now and then you'd have to like, 'balance' it, by basically doing a bunch of math. Thankfully, we don't need to do that any more, as we now have A.I. to help with a lot of the stuff in the finance sector. A.I. can analyze financial trends, predict stock prices and even detect fraud faster than any human could.

Marketing: A.I. helps marketing folk figure out what it is that people want to buy and when they most likely want to buy it. Ever wonder why you keep seeing ads for those shoes you looked at, once, like maybe two weeks ago? That's A.I. at work, tracking your preferences and making sure companies know exactly what you're into.

Customer Service: No one likes to be on hold with customer service - for one, their hold music always sucks. That's where A.I.-powered chatbots come in to rescue us. They can answer common questions, solve simple problems and direct more significant or trickier issues to a human person (because sometimes, you just have to talk to a real person).

A.I. + Humans = A Winning Team

One of the biggest myths about A.I. is that it's going to replace workers. In reality, A.I. is more like an assistant that helps you get through the day faster. It's there to take over the boring, repetitive tasks so you can focus on the creative, complex, or human parts of your job. Yes, companies will probably rearrange their workforce, but a lot of that is to do with them wanting to streamline or make more money. A.I. isn't trying to put anyone out of work.

For example:

I know I mention it a lot, but healthcare is like, the big thing. A.I. can analyze medical data and spot patterns that overworked doctors might miss, but at the end of the day, it's still the doctor who makes the final decision and provides care to patients, just hopefully feeling a little less overworked now they have an A.I. assistant.

In manufacturing, A.I.-powered robots can handle a bunch of repetitive tasks on the assembly line, but humans are still needed to oversee operations, solve problems and keep everything running smoothly.

What Jobs Will A.I. Create?

While A.I. might change some jobs, it's also creating new ones. As companies adopt A.I., they need people to develop, maintain and to like, improve those systems. Plus, A.I. is opening up roles that didn't even exist a few years ago, like:

A.I. Trainers: A.I. needs training, just like any new employee. A.I. trainers work to help teach systems how to recognize and understand different types of data.

Data Analysts: With A.I. generating massive amounts of data, companies need analysts to interpret that information and then figure out what to do with it.

Ethics Experts: As A.I. becomes more powerful, companies need people to make sure it's being used responsibly and ethically. These experts help ensure that A.I. systems are fair, unbiased and used for good.

The Future of Work: Working with A.I., Not Against It

As A.I. becomes a more common thing in the workplace, it's important to remember that it's a tool, not a competitor. A.I. can't replace the creativity, empathy and problem-solving skills that like, a regular human can bring to the table. Instead, it's here to handle the tasks that can be automated, freeing up humans to focus on the things that truly require human ingenuity (and maybe even provide a little extra free time for some binge-watching!)

In the future, we'll see more workplaces where A.I. and humans work side by side. The best part? A.I. can help reduce job burnout, a genuinely serious problem these days, by taking over the boring tasks, allowing us to focus on the work we find the most meaningful.

TL/DR:
A.I. isn't here to take your job - it's here to help you do your job better. Whether you're working in finance, healthcare, marketing or manufacturing, A.I. is already part of the team. It handles the repetitive, data-heavy tasks while you get to focus on the creative and critical thinking that makes your work uniquely human. The workplace of tomorrow isn't about robots taking over; it's about A.I. and humans working together, each doing what we do best.

CHAPTER 6: ENHANCING HUMAN CREATIVITY WITH A.I. (BECAUSE TWO HEADS ARE BETTER THAN ONE)

When most people think about the idea of 'creativity', they imagine a lot of the old-school painters, writers, musicians - basically humans coming up with brilliant ideas out of thin air. But here's a surprise: A.I. is actually really good at helping people get creative. Don't worry, it's not going to like, write your next novel before you get the chance, but A.I. can help us think in new ways, inspire fresh ideas and maybe even assist in creating some amazing works of art.

How A.I. Helps Creativity: The Not-So-Starving Artist

A lot of people might consider A.I. and creativity to be complete opposites. How can a machine that relies on data and algorithms possibly be creative, especially when I've repeatedly said that humans are the creative ones? Well, A.I. isn't creative in the same way that humans are. It could even be argued that what A.I. does isn't technically creative - it is great at analyzing patterns, generating possibilities and combing through data, so A.I. creation is more like an analysis of input rather than creativity as we know it. It won't replace your imagination, but it can definitely help kickstart it.

Here are a few examples of how A.I. boosts creativity across different fields:

Art: A.I. can help artists create new styles or discover interesting patterns. Programs like DeepArt use neural networks to transform photos into paintings in the style of famous artists like Van Gogh or Picasso. Is it replacing the artist? No. It's giving artists a tool to experiment with and see things in a new way.

Music: A.I. isn't composing the next hit single, but it's really good at helping musicians experiment with sounds. A.I. can analyze existing songs, find patterns in melodies and even suggest chord progressions or beats.

Writing: A.I. can't write a bestselling book on its own, but it can help with things like brainstorming, structuring ideas, or even editing. Some writers use A.I. to overcome writer's block by making suggestions, while others use it to type as they speak (wink wink).

A.I. in Design: More Than Just some Fancy Tool

A.I. is also a big player in design. From fashion to architecture to web design, A.I. is helping creators make more innovative and efficient decisions. Instead of doing all the work, A.I. works as a co-creator, like helping to streamline processes, analyze trends and suggest creative solutions. It can analyze designs and plans, run through hypothetical scenarios etc to spot issues that human designers may have overlooked.

For example:

Fashion design: A.I. can analyze like, tons of data to predict upcoming trends, helping designers stay ahead of the curve. Plus, A.I. can help design clothing by suggesting new fabric patterns or combinations that a designer might not have considered, as well as suggesting possible issues that the designer might not have taken into consideration. "Single line stitching in those new yoga pants? Girl, for those motions you're gonna want to double that up!"

Architecture: A.I. can assist architects in designing buildings by generating potential structures, optimizing materials, testing different weather scenarios, spotting structural weaknesses and even suggesting the best ways to improve energy efficiency. Don't worry -

the final blueprints still need a human touch.

The Future of Creative Collaboration: Humans and A.I.

If A.I.'s good at analyzing patterns and generating ideas and humans are good at making judgment calls, thinking outside the box and creativity, then together, we make a pretty great team. Instead of worrying that A.I. will like, replace artists, musicians, or writers, we should see A.I. as a pretty awesome creative partner, pushing our imaginations further than we thought possible (and checking our work for things we might have missed).

Here are some ways humans and A.I. are already teaming up to create:

A.I.-assisted film editing: A.I. can speed up the editing process by identifying key moments in hours of footage. Directors still make the final cuts, but A.I. can help save time.

A.I.-powered photo editing: Tools like Adobe Photoshop use A.I. to make photo editing faster and more intuitive. Want to remove like, the background of an image, or you think you look pretty good but your ex is in the picture? A.I. can sort it in seconds, letting you focus on the creative stuff.

A.I. Won't Replace Human Creativity, It'll Amplify It

One of the best things about A.I. is that it doesn't have human limitations. It doesn't get tired or distracted, it doesn't need breaks or a snack and it can process tons of information in like, seconds. But what it lacks is exactly what makes us humans unique - our ability to think emotionally, intuitively and creatively.

So, instead of seeing A.I. as a replacement for human creativity, we should see it as an amplifier. It helps us take our creative ideas and push them to 11, helping us explore new possibilities we might not have thought of on our own.

TL/DR:
A.I. is helping humans get creative in ways we've never imagined. Whether it's art, music, writing, or design, A.I. isn't replacing the creative process, it's just enhancing it. With A.I. as our partner, we can dive deeper into creativity, push the limits of what we can create and maybe even come up with some of the most exciting ideas we've ever had.

CHAPTER 7: A.I. IN SCIENTIFIC DISCOVERY AND RESEARCH (YOUR NEW LAB PARTNER)

If you think of scientists as geeks in lab coats, surrounded by lots of glass equipment and doing lots of math, you might be in for a surprise; A.I. is quickly becoming an essential part of scientific research. Just like a trusty lab partner who helps you run your experiments, analyze data and even come up with new ideas, A.I. is changing the way scientists work and discover new things.

How A.I. Is Shaking Up Science

Imagine trying to find a needle in a haystack. Now imagine that the needle is a cure for some disease and that the haystack is like, a mountain of data. That's where A.I. comes in. Scientists are dealing with more information than ever before - literally billions of data points from all sorts of experiments, clinical trials and observations. A.I. helps sort through this massive amount of data, looking for patterns and insights that would take a team of humans possibly years to find.

Here are some specific ways A.I. is becoming a big player in the world of science:

Drug Discovery: One of the most exciting areas of A.I. in healthcare is drug discovery. Traditionally, developing a new drug could take years, cost millions of dollars and might not be viable in the long run. With A.I., researchers can analyze how different compounds interact with a disease and with our bodies much faster. A.I. can even predict which compounds are the most likely to succeed before any testing even occurs. It's like being a pharmaceutical research psychic!

Genomics: This is studying the DNA of something, often humans, for medical reasons. In the field of genomics, A.I. helps scientists analyze genetic information at like, pretty much literal lightning speed. By examining genetic sequences, A.I. can help spot mutations that may lead to diseases, paving the way for personalized medicine that custom designs treatment to each individual's genetic makeup. Imagine getting a treatment plan that's as unique as your DNA!

Climate Science: Climate change is one of the biggest challenges we face today, no matter how many powerful people try to pretend it's not real. Thankfully, A.I. is helping scientists model and predict climate patterns. A.I. can analyze like, crazy amounts of climate data to find trends and make more accurate predictions about the future. It effectively reads the Earth's medical data and helps us make better decisions to treat and protect it.

A.I. and the Scientific Method: A New Twist

You will remember the 'scientific method' from your high school science class: ask a question, do some research, form a hypothesis, conduct an experiment, analyze the results, check to see if your hypothesis was right and then answer the question based on the results. A.I. is not here to replace this method but to enhance it. Here's how:

Hypothesis Generation: Instead of starting from the beginning, scientists can use A.I. to skip ahead a bit and generate hypotheses based on existing data. A.I. can analyze what has already been studied and suggest new areas for exploration.

Data Analysis: Analyzing data can be super time-consuming, kinda dull and also like, crazy complicated. A.I. tools can quickly figure out trends and correlations in the data, allowing scientists to focus on interpreting results rather than doing the math.

Automation of Experiments: A.I.-powered robots can automate all sorts of everyday laboratory tasks, like mixing chemicals or conducting tests. This frees up scientists to focus on other things, like figuring out how to save the world, one experiment at a time.

The Human Touch: Why We Still Matter

While A.I. is transforming science, let's not forget the human element. A.I. may be able to analyze data faster than any human scientist, but it lacks intuition, empathy and like, the creative spark that humans bring to research. Scientists still need to design the experiments, interpret results and make ethical decisions.

For instance, while A.I. can suggest potential drug candidates, it's the researchers who understand the implications of those drugs, including safety and efficacy. Humans ask the big questions that A.I. simply can't.

Collaboration: Humans and A.I. as Research Partners

In the world of science, the best results come from teamwork. A.I. isn't here to replace scientists; it's here to be their partner. Together, humans and A.I. can tackle some of the most pressing challenges facing our world. Maybe one day we'll see a future where scientists are freed from the burdens of data analysis, allowing them to focus on creative problem-solving and groundbreaking discoveries. With A.I. by their side, researchers can push the boundaries of what's possible.

TL/DR:
A.I. is revolutionizing scientific discovery in ways that were once unimaginable. From drug discovery to climate research, A.I. is helping scientists uncover answers faster and more efficiently. While A.I. may be quick and pretty smart, the human aspect is irreplaceable, ensuring that research remains meaningful and ethical. As we move forward, the bonds between humans and A.I. will only strengthen, allowing us

to tackle whatever drama the future brings with creativity and good ideas. So, the next time you think of a scientist in a lab, remember, it might just be their A.I. assistant!

CHAPTER 8: A.I. AUGMENTING HUMAN ABILITIES (A SUPERPOWER FOR EVERYONE)

You know when you're trying to solve a problem and you wish you had a bit more brainpower to get you there quicker? Well, that's basically what A.I. can do for humans - it boosts our abilities, making us faster, smarter and, as I mentioned earlier, even more creative. Think of A.I. as a kind of superpower that helps us do things we couldn't do on our own.

What Does 'Augmenting Human Abilities' Even Mean?

To 'augment' something means to make it better or stronger. In this case, A.I. helps us improve our thinking, decision-making and our creativity. It doesn't replace us; it just helps us do what we're already good at, just faster and more efficiently.

Here's how A.I. is like a superpower for different kinds of abilities:

Cognitive Abilities: A.I. can help us think better by analyzing huge amounts of information quickly and suggesting new ideas or like, solutions to things.

Creative Abilities: From music and art to writing and design, A.I. can boost our creativity by offering suggestions or helping us experiment with new ideas.

Problem-Solving Abilities: A.I. is great at solving complicated problems by looking at lots of data and finding patterns we might not notice or don't have time to look through.

A.I. as Your Thinking Assistant - A Watson To Your Holmes

Let's say you're trying to figure out the best way to plan a festival. There are like, a million things to consider - food, the venue, what bands will play, how much tickets will cost etc. It's a lot to manage and we've all seen the stories of how bad a badly planned festival can go! A.I. can help you by analyzing all the options and giving you recommendations.

Some examples of how A.I. helps with thinking and decision-making:

Doctors use A.I. to help diagnose diseases by analyzing medical records and symptoms. A.I. might suggest possible causes for a patient's illness, but the doctor makes the final decision.

Business leaders use A.I. to analyze like, market trends and things, helping them decide what products to sell, when to sell them or where to open new stores.

A.I. Creates A More Creative You

Creativity isn't just about things like painting or writing. It's about coming up with new ideas and solving problems in clever ways. A.I. can help ignite that creativity by like, suggesting new approaches or maybe offering ideas we hadn't considered.

Problem? A.I. Can Solve It!

A.I. is also a problem-solving powerhouse. It's great at looking at complex situations, finding patterns and suggesting solutions. While humans are still in charge of making decisions, A.I. can point us in the right direction, saving us time and energy.

Here's how A.I. helps:

In education we often use A.I. to help analyze how students learn and suggest personalized learning plans that will help each student succeed.

In science, A.I. helps researchers analyze data from experiments, speeding up discoveries and allowing scientists to focus on the big picture.

Humans + A.I. = The Ultimate Dream Team

The best part about A.I. is that it works with us, not against us. Humans bring creativity, intuition and judgment to the table, while A.I, brings speed, data analysis and powerful problem-solving skills. Together, we can do more than we ever could alone - A.I. doesn't take away what makes us human - it like, super enhances it.

TL/DR:
A.I. is helping humans think faster, create better and solve problems like we could never do before. It's like a superpower, boosting our natural abilities to help us reach our full potential. The best part? We're still in control and A.I. is just here to lend a hand whenever we need it.

CHAPTER 9: A.I. AND ETHICS—NAVIGATING CHALLENGES TOGETHER (BECAUSE EVEN SUPERPOWERS NEED RULES)

As amazing as A.I. is, it also brings up some important questions that often lead to drama. How do we make sure A.I. is used for good? How do we protect people's privacy and avoid bias in A.I. decisions? These are the big, tricky questions, but they're important ones that we need to figure out as A.I. becomes more powerful.

Think of it like this: A.I. is a powerful tool, but just like with any tool, we need to use it sensibly. You probably wouldn't give a toddler a hammer, just like we shouldn't let A.I. do whatever it wants without setting some ground rules.

Why Do Ethics Matter in A.I.?

Ethics is all about deciding what's right and wrong, fair and unfair. When it comes to A.I., ethical questions help us make sure that this technology benefits everyone, not just the rich and powerful. Since A.I. is being used in more and more areas of life, it's appearing in areas where we humans typically like a bit of privacy - healthcare, finance, even policing, so we need to be careful about how it's designed and how it's used.

For example, A.I. can help police find criminals by analyzing crime data, but like, if the data it's based on is biased, it could unfairly target certain groups of people and things are bad enough already. That's where ethics come in - helping us make sure A.I. is fair and doesn't harm anyone.

Privacy Matters: Keeping Your Information Safe

One of the biggest concerns with A.I. is privacy, because A.I. systems often need lots of data to work well. For example, your phone's A.I. assistant learns how to respond to your voice by collecting data on how you speak. But this raises the question: who has access to all that data and how is it being used?

Here's how A.I. and privacy come into play:

Data collection: A.I. relies on mega amounts of data to make smart decisions. Who owns that data? Where did it come from? How is it stored and protected? These are the kinds of questions A.I. companies need to think about.

Informed consent: People need to know how their data is being used. Whether it's like, your shopping habits or your medical history, you should have the power to decide what information gets shared and who can use it.

Bias in A.I: When Fairness Gets Messy

A.I. is only as good as the data it's trained on, which means if the data has biases, the A.I. can end up making unfair decisions. For example, if an A.I. system is trained on biased hiring data, it might unfairly favor certain candidates over others. This is a big deal, especially when A.I. is being used to make important decisions, like who gets a loan or who gets hired for a job.

To avoid this, companies are working on ways to make A.I. more transparent and accountable, so we can spot and fix these biases before they cause harm.

Accountability: Who Do We Blame When A.I. Makes a Mistake?

A.I. is powerful, but it's not perfect. Sometimes, A.I. systems make mistakes - like suggesting a really terrible song on your playlist or worse, making an unfair decision in a hiring process. The big question is: who's responsible when A.I. messes up?

Humans in charge: A.I. may make recommendations or help automate tasks, but at the end of the day, humans are still responsible for making the final decisions. It's up to us to make sure A.I. is used fairly and ethically.

Building Trust: A.I. Needs to Earn It

If A.I. is going to be part of our lives, it needs to earn our trust. That means being transparent about how A.I. works, making sure it's used responsibly and protecting people's privacy. Companies and governments need to work together to create like, actual ethical guidelines that ensure A.I. benefits everyone, not just a select few.

Here's how we can build trust in A.I.:

Explainable A.I.: People need to understand how A.I. makes decisions. If A.I. recommends a treatment plan to a doctor, the doctor needs to know why that decision was made.

Fair A.I.: A.I. systems need to be fair and unbiased, which means checking for any bias in the data and making sure the A.I. doesn't discriminate against certain groups.

A.I. for Good: Using A.I. to Make the World a Better Place

A.I. isn't just about solving technical problems, it can also help solve some of the world's mega social challenges. A.I. can be used to like, fight climate change, improve healthcare and create fairer systems for everyone, but to do that we need to make sure A.I. is used ethically and responsibly.

TL/DR:
As A.I. becomes more powerful, we need to make sure we're using it in ways that help everyone. That means thinking carefully about things like privacy, fairness and accountability. A.I. is an incredible tool, but it's up to us to make sure it's used for good things. With clear rules and responsible development, A.I. can become a trusted part of our world, one that makes life better, safer and more fair for everyone.

CHAPTER 10: THE EMOTIONAL AND CREATIVE DIMENSIONS OF A.I. (CAN A.I. FEEL?)

We've talked a lot about how A.I. is smart, but what about emotions? Can A.I. feel things like happiness, sadness or love?

The simple answer is no - at least, not in the same way that we humans do.

That doesn't mean A.I. can't help us in emotional and creative spaces. As we know, A.I. is already doing some pretty impressive things when it comes to art and music, but it's also doing some awesome things in helping people manage their emotions.

Do You Love Me Back?: Can A.I. Feel Emotions?

Let's get this out of the way: A.I. doesn't have feelings. It can recognize emotions in humans (like when it detects that someone sounds happy or sad), but it doesn't actually feel anything itself. A.I. doesn't get excited about a job well done or upset when something goes wrong, it doesn't get involved with all the drama and won't get frustrated with extra work - it just processes data and follows instructions.

However, A.I. is really good at understanding emotions based on the information it's given. For example, some A.I. systems can analyze a person's voice and figure out like, if they're feeling stressed or calm. Others can read facial expressions or body language to guess someone's emotional state. It's like having a scanner that detects emotions, even if the A.I. can't feel those emotions itself.

A.I. in Art and Music: It's Getting Creative

Here's where things get interesting: A.I. may not have feelings, but it's surprisingly good at helping humans express theirs. In art, music and even writing, A.I. is being used as part of the process to create new and exciting works, obviously in collaboration with us humans.

Music: A.I. can analyze loads of music tracks and learn how different chords, rhythms and melodies work together. Musicians can use A.I. to like, suggest new sounds, create beats, or even write entire songs, with the musician's input of course. Don't worry diva, A.I. isn't stealing the spotlight. Musicians still bring the heart and soul to their music, with A.I. just helping out on the technical side.

Art: A.I. tools like DeepDream and Google's DeepArt can transform photos into artworks that mimic famous styles, like Van Gogh's or Picasso's. While A.I. can generate amazing visuals, it's the artist's vision that drives the project. A.I. just provides a new way to experiment with creativity. There has been a lot of controversy over the use of A.I. in art over the last few months and it has fueled the debate as to not only who is like, the 'creator' but also deepened the fears of artists that they'll lose their jobs. WDon't worry - while the field may change slightly, A.I. cannot create with the soul or emotion that a human can.

Writing: A.I. can help writers by generating ideas, writing prompts, taking dictation, editing or even suggesting sentence structures. It can't write the next great novel on its own (and we can tell when you've tried!), but it can make suggestions.

A.I. in Emotional Support: A.I. Can Make You Feel Good

While A.I. doesn't feel emotions, it can still help us humans manage ours. A.I.-powered mental health apps like Woebot and Wysa use chatbots to offer emotional support. These A.I. chatbots are trained to like, recognize patterns in conversations and respond with helpful advice, coping strategies or even jokes to lift someone's mood. Some could say that A.I. is able to recognize our emotions better than we can!

Obviously, these apps aren't meant to replace therapists or counselors and if you are struggling with something serious I would urge you to like, seek out professional help, or at least tell a friend or family member, but if you're just having a bad day, maybe like, spilled soda on your favorite pants, they do provide an easy, accessible way for people to get emotional support when they need it. Think of them as a friendly voice when you're having a rough day.

A.I. and Empathy: How Close Can A.I. Get?

I'm going to re-enforce this because it really is very important - A.I. can be trained to recognize emotional cues and respond in ways that seem empathetic (for example, if an A.I. system detects that someone is feeling sad, it might respond with a kind or supportive message), but it's important to remember that this is just programming. A.I. isn't really feeling empathy, it's just following patterns based on the data it's been given - while A.I. can like, simulate empathy pretty well, the real thing still comes from humans.

A.I. can help guide us, but only humans truly understand what it's like to feel something deeply and emotionally.

The Future of A.I. in Creativity and Emotions

A.I. is getting better at working in creative and emotional spaces, but it will always need humans to bring the heart, passion and creativity that make art, music and even emotional connections so special. In the future, we can expect to see more A.I. tools helping people express themselves in new ways, but the emotional core will always like, come from us.

TL/DR:
A.I. can't feel emotions, but it's great at helping us understand and

manage ours. Whether it's creating art, making music, or offering emotional support, A.I. plays an important role, but it's us humans who bring the real creativity and empathy to the table. As we continue to develop A.I., the best results will come from collaboration, where A.I. does the technical stuff and we bring the heart and soul.

CHAPTER 11: EDUCATION IN THE A.I. AGE (A.I. IN THE CLASSROOM: A + OR NEEDS IMPROVEMENT?)

Schools and classrooms are changing and A.I. is playing a big part in that transformation. From helping students learn better to making teachers' lives easier (thank you!), A.I. is becoming a valuable tool in education. But don't worry, A.I. isn't taking over the classroom - us teachers are still in charge! Instead, A.I. is here to make learning more personalized, efficient and fun.

Back To School: A.I. is Changing the Classroom

Gone are the days of one-size-fits-all education - yes it made it possible for us to teach many students something in one go, but we weren't able to personalize it to each student. A.I. is helping create more personalized learning experiences for students, making it easier for them to learn at their own pace. Whether it's through smart tutoring systems, educational apps, or adaptive learning platforms, A.I. is making education more flexible and tailored to individual needs.

Here's how A.I. is changing education:

Personalized Learning: When there is just one teacher and sometimes thirty students, it is really difficult for us to teach a subject in a way that like, connects with each student - even though, as teachers, we often know what would be the best way to teach each individual student, we literally don't have the time to make individual learning plans. A.I. systems can help by adapting lessons to each student's strengths and weaknesses. If a student is struggling with math but excelling in reading, A.I. can adjust the difficulty level, write out the math questions differently to appeal to their reading strengths and offer more practice in the areas they need help with.

Tutoring: Most of my fellow teachers and I try to offer as many tutoring hours as we can - not only does it help the students that are struggling and we really, genuinely care about each and every one's education, but, and I'll be 100% honest here, in many cases it also helps us earn a little extra which we really need! Unfortunately, we only have so many hours in the day and there are many students that require assistance.

Thankfully, A.I.-powered tutors are available 24/7 to help students with questions, homework and lessons. These tutors can provide like, instant feedback and explanations, helping students understand concepts faster. We know if you've tried to get A.I. to write your homework for you, so don't do that (it's your education, not A.I.'s - please make sure you're actually learning), but it can help you when you get stuck and need some ideas.

Grading and Feedback: Us teachers spend like, SO MUCH TIME grading papers and providing feedback. I know you hate homework, but have you ever thought about where your teachers do all that grading? Yes, at home and usually, we're not getting paid for that time. You would rather be playing games, watching Netflix, chilling out with your buddies - guess what? So would we! You write one paper one night, we have to read and grade 30 the next night! A.I. can take on some of that massive workload by grading multiple-choice questions and even giving feedback on essays. This gives teachers more time to focus on helping students learn (and also occasionally gives us enough free time to sit down for a meal with our family).

Bored of Boards? Make Learning Fun with A.I.

Remember when learning was all about textbooks and chalkboards? Maybe not, but I do - one of my classrooms when I was a kid still had like, a literal chalkboard instead of a whiteboard or a screen! Man,

I feel old! Luckily, A.I. is making education more interactive and fun through educational games, virtual labs and simulations. These tools let students explore topics in new ways, whether it's conducting virtual science experiments or solving puzzles to learn math concepts.

Gamified Learning: A.I.-powered apps turn lessons into games, making learning feel less like work and more like play. Students can earn rewards, unlock levels and compete with friends, all while learning.

Virtual Reality (V.R.) Classrooms: A.I. combined with V.R. is helping students take virtual field trips to places like ancient Egypt or outer space! Imagine learning about the solar system while 'walking' on the surface of Mars! It's not all ancient history or space though; students can take trips through like, museums and galleries around the world, allowing for international field trips, that were previously very expensive (and therefore often excluded students from lower-income families), to be experienced without ever leaving the classroom!

Helping Teachers Be Superheroes (Let Me Grab My Cape!)

A.I. isn't just helping students - as I've already mentioned, it's making our lives as teachers easier too. By taking care of some of the more time-consuming, repetitive tasks, like grading or tracking student progress, A.I. gives teachers more time to focus on what we do best: teaching and connecting with students.

Classroom Management: A.I. can help teachers keep track of attendance, grades and student behavior, allowing them to focus on what really matters - helping students succeed. This used to require a whole lot of paperwork/data entry, but now several places have simplified the process with A.I. systems.

Customized Lesson Plans: This is used more in small classrooms and private schools, where the teachers have less students and are able to focus more on the individual, but many of us use it to help with tutoring. A.I. can suggest lesson plans based on each student's progress and like, their learning style. This helps teachers offer more personalized attention without us spending hours on preparation.

Wait For It! Preparing Students for the A.I.-Powered Future

As A.I. becomes more common in the workplace, students need to be prepared for a future where they'll be working alongside A.I. in everyday environments. Schools are starting to teach skills like coding, data analysis and critical thinking to help students thrive in an A.I.-powered world.

STEM Education: More schools are focusing on science, technology, engineering and math (STEM) subjects to help students understand how A.I. works. Learning these skills will be key for future careers in industries like tech, healthcare and engineering.

A.I. Literacy: Just as students need to learn how to read and write, they'll also need to understand how A.I. works. This is one of the areas I like to teach specifically and it includes learning about algorithms, data privacy and like, how to use A.I. responsibly.

The Human Touch: Teachers Are Still #1 (Yay!)

While A.I. is a great tool for learning, it will never replace the importance of human teachers. You might not always believe it, but we genuinely try to bring empathy, creativity and the ability to understand students to the job everyday, in ways that A.I. just can't. We work hard to build relationships, inspire curiosity and to like, help students navigate not just their studies, but life. A.I. can assist, but it's us teachers who turn lessons into something meaningful and memorable.

TL/DR:

A.I. is changing education for the better, making learning more personalized, fun and efficient. It's helping students succeed and giving teachers more time to focus on what really matters. But while

A.I. is a powerful tool, it's the combination of smart technology and dedicated teachers that like, creates the best learning environment. The future of education is bright and with A.I. and teachers working together, students have more opportunities than ever before.

CHAPTER 12: A.I. FOR GOOD: SOCIAL IMPACT AND SUSTAINABILITY (SAVING THE WORLD, ONE ALGORITHM AT A TIME)

While I've covered parts of this chapter several times so far, I want to like, really focus in on the really great things that A.I. is doing for us and our world because it is something that really does affect us all. When most people think about A.I., they imagine robots or like, smart assistants, helping us humans with our everyday tasks. They're not wrong, but A.I. is also being used to tackle some of the world's biggest challenges, from fighting climate change to improving healthcare. It's not just about making our lives easier, it's about making the world better.

A.I. and Climate Change: A High-Tech Solution

Even those that used to deny climate change is a thing are having to reevaluate their stance as our world changes and we see more frequent extreme weather events. Climate change is one of the most pressing issues we face today and A.I. is stepping up to help. A.I. can analyze huge amounts of environmental data and make predictions about like, future climate patterns. It's also being used to come up with solutions that help reduce pollution and protect the environment.

Here's how A.I. is helping with sustainability:

Predicting Climate Patterns: A.I. can analyze data from satellites, weather stations and even social media to predict how the climate might change in the future. This helps scientists and governments plan for things like natural disasters, rising sea levels and extreme weather.

Reducing Energy Use: A.I. is being used to make buildings, cities and even factories more energy-efficient. For example, smart thermostats can learn when to heat or cool a building based on when people are there, saving both energy and money.

Monitoring Deforestation: I'm going to go on a small rant here because this is something that like, really bugs me! People don't realize the huge problems deforestation causes. Trees are a vital part of the ecosystem, not only providing a home to flora and fauna, but in many places, tribes of like, indigenous people.

I'm sure you're aware from any basic science class that, through photosynthesis, trees take in carbon dioxide (the stuff that we breathe out) and release oxygen (the stuff we breathe in). We can't breathe carbon dioxide, we would suffocate and die, so we're very fortunate that trees turn it back into oxygen. Cutting down trees stops them producing oxygen and burning the wood from trees for fuel (one of the main reasons for deforestation) releases more carbon dioxide. Even if you don't account for all of the great things living trees do, it's important to remember - less trees means there is less oxygen.

Thankfully, A.I.-powered drones and satellites can monitor forests and track deforestation in real-time. This helps governments and environmental groups take quick action to stop illegal logging and helps keep the human race alive a little longer.

A.I. in Healthcare: Saving Lives, Stat!

One of my favorite areas of A.I. development is healthcare, as you'll have probably picked up on! A.I. isn't just helping the planet, it's like, literally saving lives, my Dad's being one of them.

In healthcare, A.I. is being used to diagnose diseases faster, create personalized treatment plans and even predict future health problems. By analyzing medical data, A.I. helps doctors make better decisions and catch problems earlier.

Here are a few ways A.I. is changing healthcare:

Early Diagnosis: A.I. can analyze medical images, like X-rays or MRIs and detect early signs of diseases like cancer. This means patients can get treatment sooner, improving their chances of recovery. It was thanks to an early A.I. diagnosis that my Dad was able to get treated for his cancer before it spread, which not only made me love A.I. more, but made my Dad appreciate what I teach!

Predicting Health Risks: By looking at data from a person's medical history, A.I. can predict future health issues. For example, A.I. can warn doctors if a patient is at risk of developing heart disease or like, diabetes, allowing them to take preventive action.

Personalized Treatment Plans: A.I. can help doctors create treatment plans based on a patient's unique needs, ensuring they get the best possible care. It's like having a custom-tailored healthcare plan just for you.

Fighting Poverty with A.I.: A Hero For Us All

A.I. is also being used to fight poverty and to like, improve living conditions for people around the world. By analyzing data on things like income, education and access to resources, A.I. helps governments and organizations identify where help is needed most.

Some examples include:

Improving Access to Education: A.I.-powered apps can provide educational resources to people in remote or underserved areas, giving them access to learning opportunities they wouldn't have otherwise.

Disaster Relief: When disasters like earthquakes or floods strike, A.I. can quickly analyze data to identify the hardest-hit areas, helping relief teams provide aid more effectively.

It is Only Fair To Make A.I. Fair (and Inclusive)

While A.I. has the potential to do a lot of good, it's important to make sure that it benefits everyone, not just a few people. That's why researchers and developers are working to make A.I. more fair, inclusive and accessible to all.

Here are a few ways A.I. is being used for social good:

Fighting Bias: Unfortunately, humans tend to have some bias, whether we're conscious of it or not. Because of this, A.I. systems can sometimes be biased if they're trained on like, biased data. Researchers are working to identify and eliminate bias in A.I., ensuring that everyone is treated fairly.

Accessible Technology: A.I. is helping create technology that's more accessible for people with disabilities. For example, A.I.-powered speech recognition can help people who are visually impaired navigate things like the internet and voice-activated assistants make it easier for people with mobility challenges to control their devices.

The Future of A.I. for Good

While it is the experience that most of us have with A.I. on a daily basis, it isn't just about our convenience. The future of A.I. is about using technology to make the world a better place. As A.I. continues to advance, we can expect even more breakthroughs in healthcare, sustainability and social impact.

TL/DR:

A.I. isn't just about like, the smart gadgets and the high-tech tools, it's also a powerful force for positive change. Whether it's helping fight climate change, saving lives in healthcare, or improving education and accessibility, A.I. is being used to solve some of the world's toughest challenges. As we continue to develop and refine A.I., the possibilities for good are endless.

CHAPTER 13: THE LIMITS AND DANGERS OF ARTIFICIAL INTELLIGENCE - DO NOT DO THAT ALONE!

Chapter 13 - unlucky for some!

A.I. has already done some incredible things, but with great power comes great responsibility. We know that A.I. can make our life easier, it can help save lives, nurture our creativity and solve complex problems, but it's important to remember that it is not perfect. Yes, it might be programmed by humans to do a specific task, but it doesn't have the ability to think beyond its scope like we do, to have empathy, to doubt or reconsider and so it can be dangerous when used the wrong way.

This chapter isn't here to like, scare you or anything - A.I. is a great tool for humans and we can work together to do great things, but it is also important to look at the things we shouldn't use A.I. for, the need for human oversight and why it's important to set limits.

Spoiler alert: it's not just because A.I. running things by itself is risky, but because when it goes wrong, it can go really wrong.

A.I. in War: Robots Shouldn't Decide Who To Terminate

Imagine robots in a war zone, making decisions about who to target and when to attack, all without a human in control. Sounds like we're back to the Terminator, right? But in real life, this is something that some governments around the world are trying to work on.

A.I.-controlled weapons, officially called autonomous weapons, use their A.I. programming to make combat decisions. The problem? A.I. doesn't understand human values or emotions. We know that A.I. can process a lot of data really quickly, but it can make mistakes. What happens if like, it makes the wrong choice and attacks innocent people? Worse yet, what if these weapons get hacked or malfunction? They could potentially cause massive destruction without anyone being able to stop them.

That's why a lot of experts say we should never let A.I. control weapons by itself. People need to be in charge of life-and-death decisions, not machines.

A.I. Spy: Why Constant Surveillance is a Bad Idea

We know that some companies are using A.I. to watch what people purchase and when, but there are some governments and unpleasant companies that also want to monitor what people do, both online and in real life. This isn't the harmless marketing systems, helping you to find and purchase items, like a pinball machine, you didn't even know you needed. This is the sinister type of watching, the kind that invades your privacy, know who you talked to, about what, when and all the gossip you shared.

While there are some really fun and helpful things that facial recognition apps can do, there are places where cameras, powered by A.I. can recognize people's faces, track where they go and even predict their actions. While this is really helpful for catching criminals and keeping us safe, it can be super creepy and dangerous if it is misused.

For example, in some countries, this kind of A.I. is used to track people who protest or speak out against the government. It can lead to punishments for just like, expressing your opinions. Even in places where it's meant to be helpful, like in airports, A.I. can get it wrong. These systems sometimes mix up who people are and that could mean being wrongly accused of something you didn't do. While a human could no doubt be able to check things through and clear anyone who is innocent, it would still be an unpleasant experience and likely cause you serious delays!

There is a fine line between keeping us safe and spying on us - A.I. surveillance needs to be carefully controlled by humans and only deployed where necessary.

Pick Me, Pick Me! A.I. Picking Who Gets the Job

Imagine applying for your dream job and you find out that the first thing to look at your resume isn't a person, but an A.I. program. It sounds efficient - after all, A.I. can sort through hundreds of resumes like, super fast. But, as I've mentioned before, there's a problem: A.I. can have biases if they were trained with biased data.

For example, if a company's A.I. has been trained using past hiring data and that company has mostly hired men before, the A.I. might think that men are the better candidates for jobs, just because that's what the data that it learnt from showed. This is genuinely a real life thing that happened at a big tech company - the A.I. started favoring male applicants because the system learned from biased data.

Once again we return to the very important message - A.I. works best with human teamwork and it is very important to check the training data is unbiased.

Deepfakes: Is This The Real Life, Or Is It Just Fantasy?

I'm sure we've all seen a video of someone saying something crazy, shocking or super hilarious, only to find out later that it was totally fake. A.I. can now create deepfakes, which are like, super-realistic videos where someone's face or voice is swapped to make it look like they said or did something they didn't actually do/say.

While most of these deepfakes are made for fun or harmless pranks, others can be used for dangerous reasons. Imagine a deepfake video of a world leader saying something that could cause panic or start a conflict. Or even worse, someone could use a deepfake to spread some drama about another person, damaging their reputation or getting them into serious trouble.

Since deepfakes are getting harder to spot, it's becoming more difficult to trust everything we see online. That's why using A.I. to make deepfakes can be really harmful, especially when it's done to spread lies or hurt people. As with everything we humans have created, the nature of A.I. will depend on the human using it. That is why we all have a responsibility to do our best to like, make this world better!

A.I. All Alone With Big Decisions

Lots of companies use A.I. to help them make big decisions, like whether someone can get a loan or how much they should pay for insurance. While it is so much faster to have A.I. process all the data, humans should always be the ones to make all the final decisions. While this seems really obvious, we've actually learned it from making mistakes.

For example, a healthcare organization here in the US tried to automate their entire system, believing that it could save them a lot of money. However, the A.I. system learned from some seriously messed up, biased data. Of course, the A.I. didn't know that there is bias in the data it was taught from, so it just did what it was programmed to do, resulting in an incredibly unfair and unjust system. It not only cost them a lot of money to fix it, but the damage that was done to their reputation was intense!

Once again, a great example of why humans and A.I. need to work together, with A.I. churning through all the time-consuming data and then making suggestions, while humans make the ultimate decision.

TL/DR:

A.I. is powerful, and it can do incredible things, but it's important to know where to like, draw the line. Whether it's creating dangerous weapons, invading privacy, spreading fake information or making decisions without oversight, having A.I. do everything isn't the right choice. It's up to us humans to make sure that A.I. is used responsibly and just because we can use A.I. for something doesn't mean that we should. By setting limits and using A.I. wisely, we can avoid the risks and make sure it helps the world, rather than harming it.

CHAPTER 14: SOCIETAL TRUST AND HUMAN-A.I. RELATIONSHIPS (HOW TO BE FRIENDS WITH A.I.)

As A.I. becomes a bigger part of our lives, there's one key ingredient that makes this partnership work: trust. For humans and A.I. to work well together, we need to trust the systems we use. But how do we build trust with something that isn't human? How can we make sure that A.I. is working for us and not like, secretly against us?

Trust Me Bro: Why Trust in A.I. Matters

Trust is important in any relationship, whether it's between partners, friends, coworkers, or in this case, humans and A.I. systems. If people don't trust A.I., they won't use it and that could slow down the positive changes that A.I. can like, bring to our whole society. However, if people trust A.I. too much without understanding how it works, that can lead to problems too.

So, what does trust in A.I. look like?

It means understanding how A.I. makes decisions, making sure A.I. is fair and unbiased and being transparent about how A.I. systems are designed and used.

How Do We Build Trust in A.I.?

Building trust in A.I. isn't all that different from building trust between people. It takes time, honesty and like, open, clear communication. Here's how we can make sure people feel confident using A.I.:

Transparency: People need to know how A.I. works. If an A.I. system is helping to make big decisions (like in hiring, healthcare or policing), people have the right to understand what factors the A.I. is considering. It's like when you try to explain your thought process before giving a friend some advice.

Accountability: A.I. systems might be like, super powerful, but they're still created by us regular humans. That means we need to hold companies and developers accountable for making sure their A.I. systems are fair and safe. If something goes wrong, there should be clear rules about who is responsible.

Fairness: For A.I. to be trusted, it has to be fair. That means making sure A.I. isn't biased against certain groups of people. Bias can like, accidentally sneak into any A.I. system if they're trained on biased data, so it's important to constantly check and correct for that.

Humans + A.I. = A Balanced Partnership

In many cases, A.I. helps make decisions, but humans still have the final say. This balance between humans and A.I. is key to building trust. It's like working with your smart assistant: it can offer advice, crunch the numbers or find a song you've got stuck in your head, but in the end it's humans that bring in the creativity, empathy and intuition to make the final decision and decide what's right.

A reminder of the examples we have looked at previously (repetition = memory):

In healthcare, A.I. can analyze medical data and suggest potential diagnoses, but it's the doctor who reviews the information and decides on the best course of action.

In business, A.I. can analyze market trends and suggest investment strategies, but it's up to the human team to decide which risks are worth taking.

By working together, A.I. and humans can make better decisions than either could alone.

Trusting A.I. in Everyday Life (Because That's What We Do Every Day)

We already trust A.I. in many parts of our lives, often without even realizing it. We might know that voice assistants like Siri or Alexa, or the algorithms that suggest what to watch on Netflix are controlled by A.I., but how many of us have stopped to realize that like, we now trust these everyday things without thinking about it? They are now just part of our lives. We rely on A.I. to make our lives easier and more efficient, but as A.I. becomes more involved in important areas like healthcare, education and justice, it's essential that we understand and trust how these systems work.

Here are some examples of how we build trust in the A.I. systems that, in previous chapters, we have already discussed are part of our everyday lives:

Smart Assistants: We trust our A.I. assistants to set alarms, check the weather or remind us of appointments. That trust is built because these systems are reliable and easy to understand.

Self-Driving Cars: These might not be that common everywhere yet, but for some, they're how they get around! Self-driving cars rely on A.I. to navigate roads, avoid obstacles and keep passengers safe. Building trust in this technology means ensuring that it's been like, really thoroughly tested and transparent about how it makes decisions.

The Importance of Being ~~Earnest~~ Ethical A.I.

For people to trust A.I., it needs to be ethical. That means A.I. systems should be taught to respect human rights, protect privacy and be designed to benefit society as a whole. Creating ethical A.I. isn't just about avoiding harm, it's about making sure that A.I. is used to improve people's lives.

TL/DR:
Trust is at the heart of every human-A.I. relationship. As A.I. becomes more powerful, it's important that we build systems that people can like, actually rely on. Transparency, fairness and accountability are key to making sure A.I. works for everyone. In the future, as A.I. continues to evolve, the most successful systems will be the ones that earn our trust, through honesty, fairness and like, a solid commitment to making the world better for all of us.

CHAPTER 15: EMBRACING THE UNKNOWN TOGETHER (THE JOURNEY AHEAD)

As we look to the future, one thing is clear: A.I. is here to stay, but instead of fearing the unknown, or kicking up drama, we have the opportunity to embrace it. Humans and A.I. are entering a new era of partnership, one that holds like, really incredible possibilities for growth, innovation and creativity. The future may be uncertain, but that doesn't mean we have to face it alone.

Punch It A.I.! The Rapid Pace of Change

Technology is evolving faster than ever before. New A.I. systems are being developed every day and they're transforming industries, solving problems and reshaping the way we live. But with all this change comes uncertainty - what will the future look like and how will A.I. fit into it?

The good news is that we don't have to have all the answers right now. The beauty of human-A.I. collaboration is that we can figure it out together. As A.I. continues to grow and adapt, so will we.

Here We Go! Facing Challenges Head-On

Of course, the journey into the future isn't without challenges. As you now know, if you've read the whole book and not just skipped to the end, we'll need to address ethical concerns, like privacy, bias and fairness, as well as ensuring that A.I. is used in ways that benefit society. But if we approach these challenges with care, thoughtfulness and collaboration, we can overcome them.

Us humans have always faced our challenges head-on and A.I. is just another tool that helps us do it better. Together, we can create a future where A.I. is not just a tool, but a trusted partner in tackling the big issues facing our world.

Innovation Through Collaboration (It's Even Fun To Say!)

One of the most exciting things about the future is the potential for innovation. With A.I. as our partner, we can push the boundaries of what's possible. Whether it's in medicine, art, science or education, A.I. can help us unlock new ideas and create solutions we've never imagined before. A.I. can process billions of ideas in like, literal seconds and offer suggestions we might never have thought of, but, as always, it's the human touch that will turn those ideas into reality.

Adaptability: The Key to Success

If there's one thing humans are great at, it's adapting to change. Throughout history, we've faced new challenges, new technologies and new ways of living and we've like, totally thrived! The journey has been incredible - from cave-people trying to figure out fire to our modern lives filled with technology. A.I. is just the next chapter in that story.

As A.I. becomes more integrated into our lives, we'll continue to learn, adapt and grow. The key to success in the future will be our ability to work with A.I., not against it. By embracing A.I. as a partner, we can ensure that the future is one of progress, not fear.

The Human - A.I. Future

While there is a lot of fear-mongering, rumors and suspicion right now, the future of humans and A.I. is one of collaboration, not competition. A.I. is here to make our lives easier, our work more productive and our creativity more expansive, but the heart of that future will always be human - the decisions we make, the creativity we bring and the empathy we share.

TL/DR:
As we move forward into the unknown, we do so with like, so much optimism and so much excitement. A.I. may be the technology of the future, but it's us humans who will shape that future. Together, we can create a world where A.I. helps us achieve more than we ever thought possible.

So, as we embrace the unknown, let's do it with curiosity, creativity and confidence, because the future is one we're building together, hand in hand with our A.I. friends.

CHAPTER 16: THE REAL LIFE STORIES OF A.I. CHANGING THE WORLD

As I hope I've demonstrated so far, artificial intelligence has been an important partner in some of the most impressive breakthroughs in science, technology and creativity. In this chapter, we'll take a look at some like, real-world stories where A.I. achieved things once thought impossible. These aren't just futuristic ideas - they're actual events that have already happened, showing us how A.I. is helping us humans in reshaping the world.

Putting the Eye in A.I. - A.I. and Retinal Scans Save Eyesight

In 2016, researchers at Google DeepMind made a major breakthrough in their medical A.I. program. They developed an A.I. system that could diagnose over 50 different eye diseases just by looking at a retinal scan, a detailed image of the back of the eye.

The story begins when the team partnered with the Moorfields Eye Hospital in the UK, which had access to like, literally more than a million eye scans. The problem they were tackling was serious, as a lot of eye diseases can lead to blindness if not treated in time, but they're hard to diagnose early.

The A.I. was trained on these images, learning to spot really, really tiny details that even the best human doctors might miss. In clinical tests, it turned out that the A.I. could diagnose these diseases as accurately as top specialists, and in some cases, even better, as A.I. doesn't get tired, stressed or distracted. Not only could the A.I. detect these conditions early, but it could also recommend the various treatments of the diseases for doctors to consider.

This breakthrough was like, a game-changer! The A.I. tool could help doctors all over the world and could make a very significant change to the quality of patient's lives, especially in areas where specialists are scarce. Thanks to A.I. and the great work by the researchers at Google DeepMind, doctors now have the chance of saving the eyesight of millions by catching diseases before they cause irreversible damage.

Listen! A.I. Writes Music: The Case of 'Daddy's Car'

A.I. isn't all about the serious stuff - there is always room for work/life balance! Ok, so A.I. doesn't have a life in that sense, but us humans can use it for creative and fun things as well as like, amazing medical breakthroughs. I don't know how many of you will remember, but way back in 2016 a unique song called 'Daddy's Car' was released. What made it special? It was composed by an A.I. called Flow Machines.

The story behind this song begins with a French composer Benoît Carré, who worked with Flow Machines to create music inspired by an old, apparently super popular, British band called The Beatles. Flow Machines wasn't just randomly generating sounds though, as it had been trained on a massive database of maybe like, thousands of songs from all different genres. When Carré, being the human, creative soul behind the project, provided the A.I. with instructions, such as the style he wanted, which in this case was a Beatles-inspired sound, Flow Machines generated a melody and chord progression based on the patterns that it learned from those songs.

Carré then took the A.I.'s creation and turned it into a finished song by arranging the music and writing the lyrics. The result was a catchy, Beatles-like tune that many listeners wouldn't guess was largely composed by a machine.

This project showed how A.I. doesn't replace humans, but can collaborate with us to push the boundaries of creativity, offering new tools for musicians and composers.

Not Playing Around - Defeating the World's Best Go Player: AlphaGo vs. Lee Sedol

Also in 2016, which was like, a HUGE year for A.I. to break boundaries, one of the biggest A.I. milestones took place when Google DeepMind's AlphaGo played against Lee Sedol, like, a truly legendary player of the ancient Chinese board game Go. What made this story so captivating was that Go is an extremely complex game - it is way more difficult than chess. Difficult as it might be to even imagine, there are more possible moves in Go than there are atoms in the whole universe.

In case you would like some additional perspective, if you write the letter 'i' in pencil, the dot you put on the top has like, 100,000,000,000,000 atoms. Basically, there are so many possibilities in GO that it makes it nearly impossible for traditional computers to 'brute force' a solution, they have to be able to think.

AlphaGo was trained not only by analyzing millions of Go games but also by playing against itself over and over and over. It seriously learned strategies that no human had ever thought of. When the match against Lee Sedol began, many experts predicted that AlphaGo would lose. Lee Sedol was considered to be like, one of the greatest players in the world and no A.I. had ever beaten a top-ranked player at Go.

But on March 9, 2016, in the first game of the match, AlphaGo stunned the world by winning. Over the next few days, it went on to win three more games out of the five-game series, with Lee only managing to win just one. The most shocking moment came in Game 2, when AlphaGo made a move that no one, including Lee Sedol, expected. The move seemed so unusual that some commentators initially thought it was a mistake, but it turned out to be like, a really brilliant and highly strategic play.

This match showed that A.I. could not only compete with human intelligence but could also surpass us in certain areas. This isn't to say that A.I. is replacing us, it will always be a partnership - AlphaGo's victory was seen as a major leap forward in A.I. research and its potential applications in helping humans with intense problem-solving.

A.I. is a Pro(tein) Predictor! Solving a 50-Year Mystery of Protein Structure

Proteins aren't just for those hitting the gym, they're essential building blocks of life, but figuring out their shape, called 'protein folding', is incredibly difficult. Scientists have spent literally decades trying to solve the structures of certain proteins, a challenge known as the 'protein-folding problem'. Knowing the shape of a protein is like, super important for understanding how it works and how to design drugs to interact with it.

In 2020, an A.I. called AlphaFold, developed by DeepMind, made a breakthrough that really amazed the scientific world. AlphaFold managed to predict the 3D structure of a protein with an accuracy that rivaled lab-based methods, which are usually super slow and mega expensive. The breakthrough came during a global competition called CASP (Critical Assessment of Structure Prediction), where AlphaFold outperformed every other team by a huge margin.

The way AlphaFold worked wasn't just cool, it was legit revolutionary. It used what we call deep learning algorithms to predict how a string of amino acids (imagine them as the Legos of building proteins) would fold into a 3D structure. This problem, which scientists had been working on for 50 years, was essentially cracked in a matter of months by AlphaFold.

The impact of this discovery is MASSIVE. Understanding protein structures more easily means faster drug development and better treatments for diseases. If there was ever a time where we needed faster drug development it was 2020, am I right? Thankfully,

AlphaFold is already helping researchers understand all sorts of diseases, not just the crazy new ones, but the nasty older ones too, like Alzheimer's and Parkinson's - with humans and A.I. working together we can speed up the creation of new medications and make like, monumental improvements to the quality of life for millions.

Hey, What's That Over There? A.I. Spots Hidden Planets: Kepler's A.I. Discovery

Space exploration isn't just trying to catch up on all the different sci-fi shows, it is also one of humanity's greatest pursuits and A.I. is playing an increasingly important role in it. In 2017, scientists at NASA used A.I. to discover two new things called 'exoplanets', which are planets that orbit stars, just like the Earth goes around our sun, but like, outside of our solar system. These planets were buried in the massive pile of data collected by the Kepler Space Telescope.

For those of you who are too young to remember, or old enough to have forgotten, the Kepler Telescope was launched by NASA in 2009 to look at the stars and gather information about what is outside of our solar system. It was active and orbiting the Earth for nine years, during which time it sent back loads of data for NASA scientists to look through.

The A.I. part of the story starts with this massive amount of data gathered by Kepler. This telescope had been observing stars for years, looking for tiny dips in brightness that could indicate a planet passing in front of them. While Kepler had found thousands of exoplanets, there was so much data that it was like, pretty much impossible for humans to go through it all. So, NASA turned to A.I. to help.

They used a neural network, which is a type of A.I. designed to recognize patterns, to analyze the data more efficiently. This A.I. had been trained to spot the signals of planets hiding in the 'noise' of the data. While analyzing this like, mountain of information, it found two new exoplanets in a distant star system, previously overlooked by human researchers.

This isn't throwing shade at the scientists and researchers at NASA - as I've said before, A.I. can process crazy amounts of information in a really short amount of time, without ever getting tired or distracted. This discovery showed that when we work together, A.I. can help us find things that we would otherwise miss, opening new frontiers in space exploration.

TL/DR:
These were just a few of the stories that highlight the power of A.I. in like, actual, real-world events. Whether it's helping a doctor save someone's eyesight, working with a composer to create a hit song, beating a world champion at a complex game, helping scientists solve a scientific mystery or digging through data to help NASA discover new planets, A.I. is making an undeniable mark on the world. This is just the beginning - who knows what future stories of A.I. and human partnerships and their breakthroughs will look like?

CHAPTER 17: BONUS! FUN AND SIMPLE A.I. PROJECTS YOU CAN TRY (NO PHD REQUIRED!)

A.I. might sound like, super high-tech and complicated, but the good news is that you don't need to be a computer genius to start experimenting with it. In fact, there are tons of easy, fun A.I. projects that you can try right now - no special equipment or advanced knowledge required. Whether you're curious about how A.I. works or just looking to try something new, these beginner-friendly projects are a great way to dip your toes into the world of artificial intelligence.

Create Your Own A.I. Art

Want to feel like a digital Picasso? A.I. art tools can help you turn your photos into stunning works of art, or even generate brand-new artwork based on your preferences. There are many free platforms where you can get creative with A.I.-generated images.

How to Try It:

Check out apps like Deep Dream Generator or DeepArt. All you have to do is upload a photo and choose a style (like Van Gogh or abstract) for the A.I. to apply to your image. Watch as the A.I. transforms your regular photo into something amazing!

Why It's Fun:

You get to explore your artistic side without needing any art skills. Plus, it's exciting to see how A.I. interprets your photos and turns them into totally new creations.

Make a Custom Chatbot

Ever wanted to create your own chatbot? You can build one to answer questions, tell jokes or even help out with simple tasks. The best part? You don't need to write any code to get started.

How to Try It:

Try using platforms like BotStar or Chatfuel to create a chatbot without coding. These tools let you drag and drop elements to create a chatbot that can respond to simple prompts or hold short conversations.

Why It's Fun:

You get to design a chatbot with your own personality and see how it interacts with others. Plus, you can amaze your friends by showing them your custom-made digital assistant.

Generate Your Own Music

If you've ever dreamed of being a music producer but don't know where to start, A.I. can help you create original tracks with just a few clicks. A.I. music generators analyze existing music patterns and create new sounds and compositions based on your input.

How to Try It:

Head over to sites like Amper Music or Soundraw. You can choose a genre, adjust the mood or tempo and let the A.I. compose a track for you. You can even tweak the music to your liking and download the final result.

Why It's Fun:

You don't need to play an instrument or have any like, music theory knowledge, just let the A.I. create the tunes! It's a great way to experiment with different sounds and even use your A.I.-generated music in videos or projects.

Play Around with A.I. Writing Tools

A.I. writing assistants aren't just for work, they can also help you have fun with creative writing. From generating story ideas to completing your sentences, A.I. writing tools can give you a hand in creating short stories, poems or even jokes.

How to Try It:

Use tools like A.I. Dungeon for storytelling adventures where you input the beginning of a story and the A.I. continues the plot based on your prompts.

Or try Rytr to help you write anything from blog posts to short creative pieces.

Why It's Fun:

You can create wild, unexpected stories with the help of A.I. and it's a great way to cure writer's block. Plus, the A.I. might surprise you with some quirky plot twists or funny lines!

Try an A.I.-Powered Language Learning App

Learning a new language can be like, so hard, but A.I. is making it easier and more fun. A.I.-powered apps can help you learn vocabulary, practice speaking and even correct your grammar.

How to Try It:

Download an app like Duolingo or Memrise, both of which use A.I.

to tailor lessons to your learning pace and style. You can practice vocabulary, grammar and conversation skills with A.I. as your tutor.

Why It's Fun:

These apps make language learning feel like a game. You can track your progress, earn points and get personalized feedback from the A.I. as you improve your skills.

Build a Face Recognition App

This one is pretty crazy and I love it! Want to see how A.I. can recognize faces? You can experiment with simple face recognition apps that like, detect and identify faces in photos or videos. It's a fun way to see how A.I. 'sees' the world.

How to Try It:

Use an online tool like Face API from Microsoft's Azure platform. You can upload photos and see how the A.I. detects faces, expressions and even emotions based on facial features.

Why It's Fun:

You get a behind-the-scenes look at how A.I. systems like facial recognition work. It's fascinating to see how accurately (or sometimes hilariously badly) A.I. can interpret different faces.

TL/DR:
These simple A.I. projects are a great way to get like, a proper hands-on experience with artificial intelligence, even if you're completely new to the concept. Whether you're creating art, making music or building your own chatbot, A.I. opens up a world of creative possibilities. So, dive in, have fun and see what amazing things you can create with the help of A.I.!

WITH THANKS!

Thank you for reading! I hope that you have found this book to be informative and helpful - if you came into this with fears of A.I., I hope I've helped relieve at least a few of those worries! I am looking forward to an exciting future, working along side A.I and I hope you are too!

Save, exit, we're done!

Lots of Love,

Ray

ABOUT THE AUTHOR

Raymond Amari

Hi everyone, I'm Raymond 'Ray' Amari and I am like, SO glad you've found (and hopefully decided to read) my book "Hey A.I." - You N' A.I. IRL! I've been obsessed with computers since I was a little kid - I must have driven my parents crazy with all my questions! This obsession turned into a career - I went to college and took all the computer classes I could find and a couple of years ago I became the computer science teacher at the local high school here in sunny California, USA.

This is an unusual book, in the sense that I worked on this with an A.I. system I created myself. I call him Greg! As I dictated the book to him, he typed it on to a screen in front of me, where I could check it was what I wanted and to highlight anything I thought was important!

I really hope that you enjoy this book, whether you're just curious about A.I., studying computer science, researching what you think might be your enemy or like, maybe just refreshing your memory from previous experiences. I know that A.I. has been such a huge topic over the last few years and there is a lot of incorrect information out there, worrying people, but I'm here to put your minds at ease!